Places We Live

Living in a
Desert

Ellen Labrecque

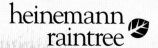
heinemann
raintree

To contact Capstone Global Library, please call 800-747-4992, or visit our web site www.capstonepub.com

Edited by James Benefield and Brenda Haugen
Designed by Richard Parker
Original illustrations © Capstone Global Library Ltd 2015
Picture research by Jo Miller
Production by Helen McCreath
Originated by Capstone Global Library Ltd
Printed and bound in China by Leo Paper Group

18 17 16 15 14
10 9 8 7 6 5 4 3 2 1

Library of Congress Cataloging-in-Publication Data
Labrecque, Ellen.
  Living in a desert / Ellen Labrecque.—1 Edition.
    pages cm.—(Places we live)
  Includes bibliographical references and index.
  ISBN 978-1-4846-0802-9 (hb)—ISBN 978-1-4846-0809-8 (pb)—ISBN 978-1-4846-0823-4 (ebook) 1. Desert people—Juvenile literature. 2. Deserts—Juvenile literature. 3. Desert ecology—Juvenile literature. I. Title.
  GN390.L33 2015
  306.0915'4—dc23   2014013628

This book has been officially leveled by using the F&P Text Level Gradient™ Leveling System.

Acknowledgments
We would like to thank the following for permission to reproduce photographs: Alamy: Barry Iverson, 21, Johner Images, 23, Robert Estall photo agency, 13; Corbis: Bob Krist, 18; Newscom: Arco Images/picture alliance/K.Kreder, 17, Danita Delimont Photography/Alison Wright, 12, Getty Images/AFP/Greg Wood, 19, Getty Images/AFP/Jamal Nasrallah, 22, Oliver Gerhard Image Broker, 11, Robert Harding/Tuul, 15, ZUMA Press/Du Boisberranger, 14; Pascal Maitre, 27; Shutterstock: apinunrin, 24, ChameleonsEye, 25, devy, cover, grebcha, 5, JuRitt, 4, Nataliya Hora, 26, Nicram Sabod, 9, p.studio66, 20, Patrick Poendl, 16, Pi-Lens, 6, prochasson frederic, 8, Xavier MARCHANT, 10.

Design Elements: Shutterstock: donatas1205, Olympus.

We would like to thank Rachel Bowles for her invaluable help in the preparation of this book.

Every effort has been made to contact copyright holders of material reproduced in this book. Any omissions will be rectified in subsequent printings if notice is given to the publisher.

Contents

Some words are shown in bold, **like this**. You can find out what they mean by looking in the glossary.

What Is a Desert?

Deserts are places on Earth that get little rainfall. Deserts get less than about 10 inches (25 centimeters) of **precipitation** a year. Deserts can be hot or cold, but many are hot during the day and cooler at night.

Some deserts can be flat land filled with sand dunes.

Some deserts have few people living in them. Other deserts have lots of people living in **settlements**. More people live in the Thar Desert in India and Pakistan than live in any other hot desert in the world.

Where Are Deserts?

Deserts are found on every **continent** and where there is little rain. The world's largest desert is the Antarctic Desert. It is made entirely of ice, and almost nobody lives there.

Most people living in the Antarctic only stay there for a short time. It's too cold to stay longer.

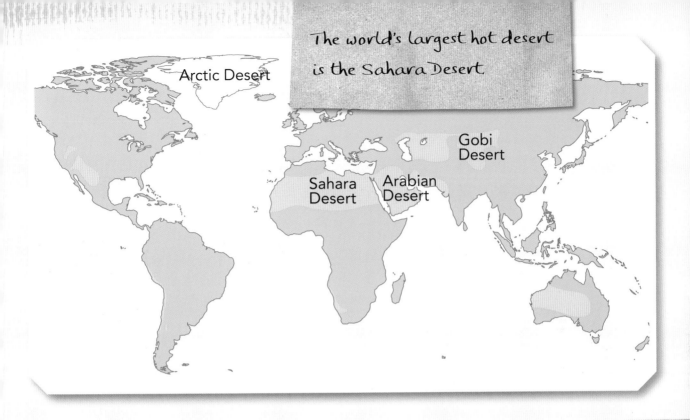

The world's largest hot desert is the Sahara Desert.

Arctic Desert

Gobi Desert

Sahara Desert

Arabian Desert

Deserts start near mountains, where clouds from the sea are stopped from moving inland by these mountains. Or deserts start where there is high **air pressure**, which stops the rain. They can also form along the coast. When warm air meets cold seas, it stops rain from coming inland.

Earth's largest deserts

1. Antarctic Desert
2. Arctic Desert
3. Sahara Desert, Northern Africa
4. Arabian Desert, Southwest Asia
5. Gobi Desert, Central Asia

All Kinds of People

Over 1 billion people live in deserts. Most of them live in cities. Cities have lots of places to work, from stores to offices. People avoid the sun and sandstorms by staying inside.

Buildings in Las Vegas, Nevada, have air-conditioning to keep people cool.

The caves of the Coober-Pedy people have no windows!

Other people live in different ways. In Africa, some people live in mud huts in the desert. In the desert in Coober-Pedy, Australia, some people live in caves. The caves help them stay cool inside when it is hot outside.

Living in the Desert

Living in the desert is tough. There is not enough rain to grow **crops**. Food and water are brought to desert cities from far away. Many desert people live near an **oasis**, where they get their water from wells.

Two-thirds of the people in the Sahara Desert get their water from wells in an oasis.

The fennec fox hunts for food at night, when the desert is not as hot

Bad weather also makes desert living hard. High winds whip up sandstorms. Dust fills the air and makes it hard to see or breathe. The animals that live there sleep during the day and roam at night.

Who Are Nomads?

Nomads move their homes from place to place. This is because they move around looking for food and water. Nomads can also travel with their own animals, such as goats and sheep.

Nomads in the Gobi Desert sleep in tents called yurts. Yurts are light to carry and easy to set up.

The Sans people suck up water through a straw.

Some nomads have unusual ways to find water. In the Kalahari Desert, Sans nomads find water under the sand. They store it in ostrich egg shells!

Weather and Clothes

In hot deserts, people wear light, loose clothes. This helps them to stay cool. People wear clothes to protect themselves, too. The Tuareg people in Africa cover their whole head with a piece of material called a **veil**.

Veils protect faces and eyes from the sun and blowing sand.

A deel can be used as a blanket. This way, nomads don't have to carry a separate blanket.

In cold deserts, people wear many layers. **Nomads** in the Gobi Desert wear long robes called deels over other warm clothes. Deels are warm because they are made from sheepskin.

15

Getting Around

Today, you can travel around most deserts in cars and trucks. Some people drive their cars off the roads. They need to be careful to not get stuck in the sand or get lost.

People should bring their own supply of food, water, and gasoline when they travel across deserts.

A camel's feet are flat and wide. This means it doesn't sink into the sand when it walks.

Many **nomads** still travel on camels in hot deserts. Camels are the perfect animal for desert travel. They have long eyelashes that help to keep sand out of their eyes. They can also go for days without food or water.

What Is School Like?

Some children in the desert go to schools like yours. Others stay at home and their mom or dad teaches them. Some children in the desert have to walk many miles to get to school.

There are many schools in the Gobi Desert.

Tests and homework at School of the Air are sent by mail or e-mail

Children who live in the Outback of Australia use School of the Air. At a School of the Air, children learn at home. They listen to teachers on a radio or watch them on a video link, using the Internet.

What Is Work Like?

Some jobs in deserts are just like jobs anywhere else. Grown-ups can be doctors or teachers and live in a desert. Sometimes just looking for food and water in the desert is a big job! But some desert jobs are special.

Some people in deserts have jobs just like the grown-ups you know.

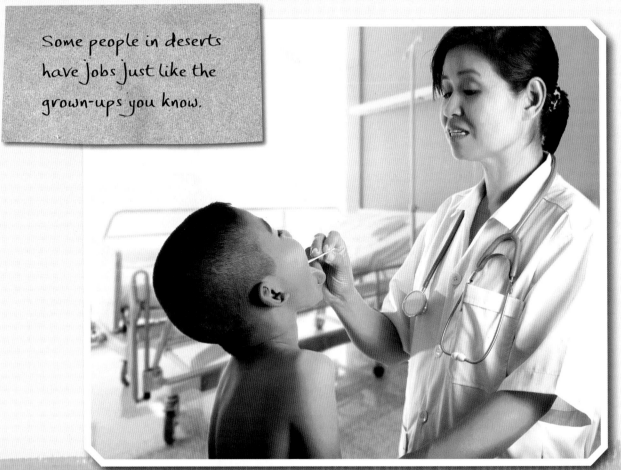

Giant pipes are used to carry oil found in the desert.

Much of the world's oil is found underneath the Arabian deserts. Workers pump the oil from the ground using special machines. Oil has many uses. For example, it can be turned into gasoline for vehicles.

Fun Things to Do

There are amazing events in deserts. Some flat deserts are perfect for speed events. The land speed record is the highest speed reached by a car. It was set in 1997 at the Black Rock Desert in Nevada, at 763 miles (1,227 kilometers) per hour!

The ThrustSSC set the land speed record.

Sandboarding is a lot like snowboarding, but on the sand.

Many people take vacations in the desert. They enjoy the hot weather and the sights. You can stay in fancy hotels with swimming pools in the Arabian Desert in western Asia. You can also try sports, such as sandboarding, in the desert.

Deserts of the Past

People have lived in deserts for thousands of years. But desert living has changed a lot. Thousands of years ago, the dry land that is now the Sahara Desert used to have lakes!

Some scientists think **climate change** has made grass, rivers, and lakes disappear.

People have also found dinosaur bones, fossilized eggs, and other fossils in the desert.

Archaeologists work in deserts to find out things about the past. They have found buildings, ancient drawings, and **artifacts** such as pottery beneath the sand.

Deserts of the Future

Some scientists say **climate change** is changing deserts. Some deserts grow bigger as land gets less rain. Other deserts grow because of **deforestation**. Without trees, land and soil dry out and blow away.

The Atacama Desert, in Chile, is growing in size every day.

We can do things to stop deserts from spreading.

People are learning to cut back on air pollution from factories and vehicles that some scientists think could cause climate change. People are also trying to **conserve** water.

Fun Facts

- Deserts have been around for millions of years.

- The most common plants in U.S. deserts are cacti. They are tough plants that have a waxy stem that holds water.

- Many reptiles live in the desert. Their scaly skin stops them from drying out in the heat.

- Most of the animals that live in hot deserts live underground!

- Sometimes tired and thirsty desert travelers see mirages of water. A mirage looks like shimmering water up ahead, but it is really just a trick (or illusion) caused by light from the sun. An illusion is something we think is real, but is not actually there.

Quiz

Are each of these sentences true or false?

1. All deserts are hot and sandy.
2. There are no cities in the desert.
3. More land is turning into desert all the time.
4. A horse is the perfect animal to ride on in the desert.
5. It is best to wear tight-fitting clothes in the desert.

5. False. Loose-fitting clothes keep you cool and protect you from the sun.

4. False. A camel is one of the best animals to travel through the desert on.

3. True. Deserts are growing every day. Some think this is because the world grows hotter and hotter.

2. False. There are many cities in the desert. Supplies are brought in from other places.

1. False. Deserts can be cold and icy. They can be rocky and full of mountains, too.

Glossary

air pressure forces that push and pull, which happen all around us, in the air we breathe. Different forces cause different weather!

archaeologist person who studies ancient people by digging up buildings and things from long ago

artifact old object made by a person. It tells us about life in a particular time.

climate change long-lasting change in the weather. Some scientists think it happens because of people causing pollution.

conserve slow down or stop something from disappearing

continent any of the world's big land areas: Africa, Antarctica, Asia, Australia, Europe, North America, and South America

crop plant grown for food

deforestation cutting down of trees and big plants, sometimes caused by having too many farm animals eating grass and plants

nomad person who has no long-lasting home. They travel from place to place to find food, water, and places to graze animals.

oasis spot in a desert where water and plants are found

precipitation mist, rain, snow, hail, or sleet that falls to the ground

settlement place where people's homes are, such as a village, town, or city

veil material that covers a face. In deserts, it protects a person from sandstorms and from the sun.

Find Out More

Books

Benoit, Peter. Deserts (True Books). New York: Children's Press, 2011.

Gaff, Jackie. I Wonder Why the Sahara Is Cold at Night and Other Questions About Deserts (I Wonder Why). Boston: Kingfisher, 2012.

Peppas, Lynn. The Atacama Desert (Deserts Around the World). New York: Crabtree, 2013.

Internet sites

Facthound offers a safe, fun way to find Internet sites related to this book. All of the sites on Facthound have been researched by our staff.

Here's all you do:

Visit www.facthound.com

Type in this code: 9781484608029

Index